British Library Cataloguing in Publication Data

Secrett, Malcolm
Successful Budgeting in a Week. -
(Successful Business in a Week Series)
I. Title II. Series
658.15

ISBN 0 340 57640 5

First published 1993

© 1993 Malcolm Secrett

Typeset by Multiplex Techniques Ltd, St Mary Cray, Kent.
Printed for Hodder & Stoughton Educational, a division of
Hodder Headline Plc, 338 Euston Road, London NW1 3BH by
Cox & Wyman Ltd, Reading, Berkshire

658.154.
SEC

Successful

~~Budgeting~~

Malcolm Secrett

Headway · Hodder & Stoughton

**British Institute
of Management**

The British Institute of Management is the leading
management institute in the UK. It is the driving
force behind the development of professional
management within the public and private sectors.
The Institute embraces all levels of management
from junior managers to chief executives and offers
a unique range of services for all management
disciplines.

If you would like to hear more about the benefits of
individual or corporate membership, please write to

Dept HS
British Institute of Management
Cottingham Road
Corby
Northants NN17 1TT

This series is commissioned by the British Institute
of Management Foundation.

■C O N T E N T S■

■ I N T R O D U C T I O N ■

Budget and cash flow forecasting is sometimes thought to be the sole domain of accountants, and remote from the practical day-to-day running of a business.

Hardly anything could be further from the truth. Budgetary forecasting relies almost entirely on a clear and pragmatic understanding of how the business works; the rest is simple arithmetic.

Being in control and seeing what decisions need to be made, well in advance, are the hallmarks of a successful manager. On the other hand, inadequate forecasting leads to hurried and reactive decisions, which are often poor and short-term. The consequences of failing to take planned and timely action can be catastrophic.

Some cynics might say that financial forecasts consume a great deal of time and are of little value. They are wrong. Properly constructed forecasts do not take long to build and maintain, they are amongst your most valuable tools, and undoubtedly provide you with a very much better understanding of your business.

The meaning of words
Wherever possible, and provided that clarity is not compromised, I have avoided 'trade jargon' and used everyday words for explanation. But of course, there are exceptions.

Many words used in accountancy are the same as those of everyday language, but with a very specific meaning. Therefore, if the best everyday word for explanation happens to be the same as the accountancy term, then I have given a definition of its specific meaning when it first becomes necessary.

Also, the terms 'he', 'him', etc. used in the book should be understood to denote both sexes.

Overview

We will start the week by familiarising ourselves with the general structure of financial forecasts.

Overview of financial forecasts
- Budgets and budget forecasts
- Cash flow forecasts
- Different types of budget and their applications

Budgets and budget forecasts

A budget is:
A statement of **allocated** expenditure and/or income, under specific headings, for a certain period.

A budget forecast is:
A statement of **expected** expenditure and/or income, based on the best information to hand, under specific headings, for a certain period.

All households have a budget, whether or not we think of them in that way. They may not be set out on paper, but we usually know how much each of the individual major items costs, such as the mortgage or rent, rates, electricity and telephone.

We probably also know when the larger of these bills will drop through the letter-box.

Before personal bank accounts were as common as they now are, people often used to put cash into several containers, or pots, marked with the item of expenditure which would be met when the need arose or the bill arrived.

The principles of a business budget are exactly the same as those for a household. We allocate the correct amount of money to each item of expenditure, bearing in mind our income. We also need to consider when the costs will arise.

This is one way in which we could set out a budget.

ITEM	WHEN	AMOUNT (£)/WHEN	TOTAL(£)
Rent	Mar, Jun	2500	5,000
Rent	Sep, Dec	2625	5,250
Rates	Mthly Mar - Dec	60	600
Electricity	Feb, May, Aug, Nov	250	1,000
Gas (Heating)	Jan	700	700
Gas (Heatng)	Apr	450	450
Gas (Heating)	Jul	100	100
Gas (Heating)	Oct	250	250
Telephone	Feb, May, Aug, Nov	650	2,600
Stationery	Monthly	75 (Average)	900
Postage	Monthly	35 (Average)	420

But there are shortcomings with this presentation.

For instance, whilst we may know what the total annual cost of an item will be, in practice it is most unlikely that it will be spread evenly between each month, and we have to resort to the use of averages as shown.

We might also want to know the total costs during a particular month. We could work it out from the table (if it were complete), but it wouldn't be very easy.

The layout on the next page overcomes these difficulties. A more realistic spread is now possible, and working out the total cost of each month is just simple addition.

BUDGET FORECAST

Expense (£)	Jan	Feb	Mar	Apr	May	Jun	Jul	Aug	Sep	Oct	Nov	Dec	Total
Rent			2500			2500			2625			2625	10250
Rates			60	60	60	60	60	60	60	60	60	60	600
Electricity		250			250			250		250			1000
Gas (heating)	700			450			100			250			1500
Telephone		650			650			650			650		2600
Stationery	50	65	100	65	65	65	65	65	190	65	65	40	900
Postage	15	25	80	25	25	25	25	25	115	25	25	10	420
Insurance				800									800
Staff training	50	150	150	150	150	75	50	50	75	125	100	75	1200
Petrol	40	25	15	25	30	35	60	125	150	125	110	75	815
Pay costs	2000	1250	750	1250	1500	1750	3000	6250	7500	6250	5500	3750	40750
Parts for widgets	4571	2857	1714	2857	3429	4000	6857	14286	17143	14286	12571	8571	93143
Total Expense	7426	5272	5369	5682	6159	8510	10217	21761	27858	21186	19331	15206	153978

Revenue (£)	Jan	Feb	Mar	Apr	May	Jun	Jul	Aug	Sep	Oct	Nov	Dec	Total
Widget sales (£)	8000	5000	3000	5000	6000	7000	12000	25000	30000	25000	22000	15000	163000
Total Revenue	8000	5000	3000	5000	6000	7000	12000	25000	30000	25000	22000	15000	163000

Cash flow forecasts

Before we look at what we can do with our budget, we must add a cash flow forecast to it. Why?

In practice many items of expenditure are obtained on a credit basis. For instance, we may have an 'account' with a supplier of stationery. Materials are obtained from them as and when they are needed, but we do not pay for them immediately. At regular intervals, usually monthly, the supplier sends an invoice for any outstanding sum owed to them. It is not unusual for suppliers to ask that their account is paid within 14 or 30 days.

In the example on the previous page there is an increase in stationery and postage costs in March, for a postal sales drive, shall we say. We take delivery of the extra stationery during March, but will not be paying for it until April.

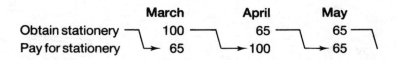

	March	April	May
Obtain stationery	100	65	65
Pay for stationery	65	100	65

Assuming similar terms from the Widget parts supplier, again we will be paying for the parts one month after we obtain and use them.

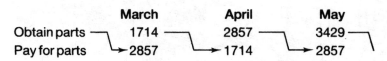

	March	April	May
Obtain parts	1714	2857	3429
Pay for parts	2857	1714	2857

If a credit card is used to buy our petrol, payment for it will also be made one month in arrears.

All through the year then, stationery, petrol and widget part supplies are paid for one month after the goods are received.

From now on, the terms **cost** or **expense** will be used to mean that cost is incurred, as for 'obtain stationery, petrol or parts'. The term **cash out** will be used to mean that the expense is actually paid, as for 'pay for stationery, petrol or parts'.

> Cost incurred = EXPENSE
> Cost paid   = CASH OUT

If petrol for a business trip is bought with a credit card, we have incurred a business **expense**. When we settle the credit card account, we have paid **cash out** of the business.

Exactly the same principle applies to income. In the example, £6000 worth of widgets are made and sold during May, but our customer does not pay us for them until June, because our sales terms are '30 days from receipt of goods'.

All through the year, then, payments for widgets are received one month after they have been made and sold.

	May	June	July
Make and sell	6000	7000	12000
Receive payment	5000	6000	7000

From now on, the term **revenue** will mean that income has been earned, as for 'make and sell'. **Cash in** will be used to mean that the sales income is actually received, as for 'receive payment'.

> Income earned   = REVENUE
> Income received = CASH IN

On a budget forecast, expense and revenue are always shown. These are both very important figures, as we will see later on, but they tell us very little about what is happening to cash in and cash out. Try using the budget to calculate cash out during October, for instance. It isn't easy.

How much cash we have in the bank is very important to us, and it is certainly of great interest to our bank manager. So we also need a forecast which shows how cash is flowing in and out of the bank account – a cash flow forecast.

A cash flow forecast is:

> A plan or estimate of cash in and cash out, for each item of expense and revenue

The structure of a cash flow forecast is very similar indeed to the budget forecast it is related to. It has to be. Cash movements occur only because of the transactions shown in the budget forecast. There are one or two exceptions to this, but we can safely ignore these for now.

The main differences that concern us now are:

1 A budget forecast shows expenses and revenue, whereas a cash flow forecast shows cash in and cash out.

Budget		**Cash Flow**	
Cost incurred	= EXPENSE	Cost paid	= CASH OUT
Income earned	= REVENUE	Income rec'd	= CASH IN

2   A cash flow forecast includes the bank balance.

The cash flow forecast overleaf is based on our budget
forecast example. There are:

Similarities
- The line headings are exactly the same.
- The period covered, Jan to Dec, is exactly the same.

Differences
- Section block headings are now CASH OUT and
  CASH IN.
- A bank account section has been added:
     C/Bal last month = Last month's closing balance
     Closing Balance = This month's closing balance.
- One month right shift of figures in lines marked*.

The lines marked with * are the items for which we have
assumed there will be a one month interval between
expense and cash out, or between revenue and cash in.

Because of these timing differences, the monthly totals in the
cash flow forecast are different to those in the budget.

You may also notice a number of other interesting features,
such as the overdrawn closing balance (shown as a minus
figure) in some months, or that the annual total of 'Cash in'
on the cash flow forecast is different to the annual 'Widget
sales' total on the budget forecast.

CASH FLOW FORECAST

Cash Out (£)	Jan	Feb	Mar	Apr	May	Jun	Jul	Aug	Sep	Oct	Nov	Dec	Total
Rent			2500			2500			2625			2625	10250
Rates			60	60	60	60	60	60	60	60	60	60	600
Electricity		250			250			250			250		1000
Gas (heating)	700			450			100			250			1500
Telephone		650			650			650			650		2600
Stationery*	40	50	65	100	65	65	65	65	65	190	65	65	900
Postage	15	25	80	25	25	25	25	25	115	25	25	10	420
Insurance				800									800
Staff training	50	150	150	150	150	75	50	50	75	125	100	75	1200
Petrol*	65	40	25	15	25	30	35	60	125	150	125	110	805
Pay costs	2000	1250	750	1250	1500	1750	3000	6250	7500	6250	5500	3750	40750
Parts for widgets*	4286	4571	2857	1714	2857	3429	4000	6857	14286	17143	14286	12571	88857
Total Cash Out	7156	6986	6487	4564	5582	7934	7335	14267	24851	24193	21061	19266	149682
Cash In (£)	Jan	Feb	Mar	Apr	May	Jun	Jul	Aug	Sep	Oct	Nov	Dec	Total
Widget sales (£)*	7500	8000	5000	3000	5000	6000	7000	12000	25000	30000	25000	22000	155500
Total Cash In	7500	8000	5000	3000	5000	6000	7000	12000	25000	30000	25000	22000	155500
Bank Account	Jan	Feb	Mar	Apr	May	Jun	Jul	Aug	Sep	Oct	Nov	Dec	Total
C/Bal last month	1500	1844	2858	1371	-194	-776	-2709	-3044	-5312	-5162	645	4584	
Cash in	7500	8000	5000	3000	5000	6000	7000	12000	25000	30000	25000	22000	155500
Cash out	7156	6986	6487	4564	5582	7934	7335	14267	24851	24193	21061	19266	149682
Closing Balance	1844	2858	1371	-194	-776	-2709	-3044	-5312	-5162	645	4584	7318	

Different types of budget and their applications

There is an infinitely broad range of environments to which budgets can be applied. For example:

- A 'costs only' departmental budget.
- A departmental budget with income.
- An entire company.
- A 'one-man' business.

A 'costs only' departmental budget. The administration department of a company, for instance, may be thought of purely as a 'cost centre', a department which expends effort and money on behalf of other departments, but which has no real income of its own.

A departmental budget with income. The sales department of a company will have expenses and revenue. It may also need to carry its share of the expenses of a 'costs only' department, such as general administration or wages.

An entire company. A large company will break its budget down into a number of departments, from which a total budget can be compiled. A smaller company may have just one budget which nevertheless embraces a number of small departments, some consisting perhaps of only one employee and their work.

A 'one-man' business. Independent professionals, self-employed contract workers, family-run corner shops or a one-man plumbing concern will usually find that a single budget and cash flow forecast is sufficient for their needs.

The nature of the business for these or any other type of budget is quite immaterial.

Whether we are responsible for a department in a large company or need to manage our own budget as an individual within the department, whether we are looking at the needs of an entire corporate entity or simply a one-man business, whether our budget contains no revenue or controls millions of pounds – **the principles are the same in any circumstance**.

It would of course be foolish to suggest that there are no differences in detail, or that some forecasts will not be more complex than others. Every application has specific and individual requirements, which determine *what* will be put in to the forecast and *how* it will be used.

The degree of complexity in the forecast, however, is determined almost solely by the size of the task which it addresses. How much that task is broken down into simpler and more manageable parts is entirely at the forecaster's discretion.

Summary

Today we have:

- discovered what a **budget** and **budget forecast** are.

A budget is:

> A statement of **allocated** expenditure and/or income, under specific headings, for a certain period.

A budget forecast is:

> A statement of **expected** expenditure and/or income, based on the best information to hand, under specific headings, for a certain period.

- understood what a **cash flow forecast** is.

A cash flow forecast is:

> A plan or estimate of cash in and cash out, for each item of expense and revenue.

- learned that a budget forecast shows **expenses** and **revenue**, whereas a cash flow forecast shows **cash in** and **cash out**.

Budget		Cash Flow	
Cost incurred	= EXPENSE	Cost paid	= CASH OUT
Income earned	= REVENUE	Income rec'd	= CASH IN

- realised that the principles of budget and cash flow forecasts apply to any sort of company or department, whatever the nature of the business or its size.

Use of forecasts and arranging the tools

Today we are going to look at:

- Uses for budget and cash flow forecasts
- Spreadsheets
- Should we use pen and paper, or a computer?
- Using a computer – where to start
- Budget and cash flow proforma on paper

Uses for budget forecasts

There are many uses for budget forecasts, for example:

- Establishing and monitoring expenditure limits
- Business planning
- Establishing the sales necessary to cover overheads
- Relating revenue to expenditure
- First estimate of profitability
- Linking costs to sales
- Business case for raising finance
- Linking to manpower planning
- Comparing overhead costs with other costs
- Cost reduction analysis
- 'What-if' analysis
- Break even assessment

Uses for cash flow forecasts

Cash flow forecasts have a more limited application than the budget forecast, indeed in some instances they may be quite unnecessary. We will be looking more closely at those cases later on. But where the budget holder is concerned with cash flow, a forecast is **absolutely essential**.

A cash flow forecast cannot sensibly exist unless there is also a budget forecast, because it is dependent upon it.

Here are some typical uses for a cash flow forecast:

- Making sure there is sufficient cash to cover expenses
- Checking that a plan will not create a cash shortage
- Optimising cash flow
- Reducing the level of cash borrowing
- Identifying the cash borrowing that will be necessary if a planned course of action is pursued

These lists are just examples of some of the more common requirements that businesses have. They are by no means exhaustive and never could be. The range of facilities available from forecasts is as wide as the need; they will do whatever we want them to.

Clearly it is necessary to construct a forecast in a way that addresses our particular requirements. We will be looking at how to do that tomorrow. In the meantime we will take a look at the tools of the forecaster's trade.

Spreadsheets

The principle tool for a forecaster is a **spreadsheet**.

A spreadsheet, whether on paper or computer, is simply a table of numbers arranged in rows and columns, upon which we can carry out arithmetic operations.

This is a spreadsheet:

Sales last year

SALESMAN	PRODUCT	Nuts	Bolts	Springs
Bloggs		2500	1500	6000
Smith		5000	2300	8250
Jones		4500	9000	—

The columns can be summed to obtain a total for each product:

Sales last year

SALESMAN	PRODUCT	Nuts	Bolts	Springs
Bloggs		2500	1500	6000
Smith		5000	2300	8250
Jones		4500	9000	—
	Totals	**12000**	**12800**	**14250**

The rows can be summed to obtain a total for each salesman:

Sales last year				
PRODUCT	**Nuts**	**Bolts**	**Springs**	**Totals**
SALESMAN				
Bloggs	2500	1500	6000	**10000**
Smith	5000	2300	8250	**15550**
Jones	4500	9000	—	**13500**
Totals	12000	12800	14250	

And finally, either the total products row or the total sales per salesman column can be summed to obtain a grand total for all products:

Sales last year				
PRODUCT	**Nuts**	**Bolts**	**Springs**	**Totals**
SALESMAN				
Bloggs	2500	1500	6000	10000
Smith	5000	2300	8250	15550
Jones	4500	9000	—	13500
Totals	12000	12800	14250	**39050**

Grand total

Incidentally, performing this 'grand total' on both the total row and the total column is a very good way of checking that there are no errors in any of the intermediate calculations.

And that is all there is to a spreadsheet. To be sure, rather more rows and columns will be used, and subtraction, multiplication and division as well as addition will be used, but this is as 'complicated' as things will get.

How can spreadsheets be produced?
A spreadsheet can be drawn directly onto paper or it can be produced using a computer.

The example we have just looked at would only take a few minutes to put on paper, but we may also want some charts which represent the figures. Like these:

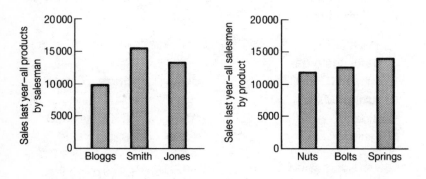

Again, simple charts like these will only take a few minutes to draw directly on paper. But if we change just one of the original figures, both of the charts would need to be redrawn.

Pen and paper or computer?

Real forecast spreadsheets will be larger than the example we have just looked at, and will probably need to be altered quite frequently for all kinds of reasons.

We will probably want more charts as well.

The old cliché 'A picture is worth a thousand words' is never more true than in the presentation of financial data. A chart ensures that the main feature of our forecast is highlighted in a way that a reader simply cannot miss.

Bear this in mind whilst we explore the pros and cons of using pencil and paper or a computer to construct forecasts and charts.

We will start with simple lists of the advantages of each:

Advantages of COMPUTER over pencil and paper
- Very much quicker
- Absolute arithmetical accuracy
- Immeasurably easier to revise
- Automatic generation of graphs
- Very easy to update regular reports
- Lower cost in the medium to long term
- Facilities which are impractical with pencil and paper
- Forecasts are more likely to be updated regularly

Advantages of PENCIL and PAPER over a computer
- Lower short-term cost if a computer is not available

Clearly there is no competition.

It is a fact of business life that most forecasts need to be updated at least once a month. A forecast which does not reflect the current status of a business is almost worthless.

A paper based system takes so much effort to maintain that we simply could not find time to update it regularly enough.

A computer based system is not only easy to update for regular maintenance, but also encourages us to test various business strategies for their impact on the budget and cash flow. This is called **business modelling**, and is just one of the many valuable advantages of using a computer.

The answers to our question 'Computer or Paper?' then are:

- If we have access to a computer with a spreadsheet, and know how to operate it - then without question we should use it.
- If we have a computer, but are unsure how to use it, then it would be best to start out using pencil and paper. This is because we do not want learning how to use the computer to impair our understanding of budgets and cash flow in the early stages. However, once we are familiar with forecasting techniques, we should then apply them to the computer.
- If we do not have access to a computer, then clearly our only option is pencil and paper.

We will now have a look at how to get started on forecasts with a computer. After that, a paper only system will be considered in case we need to start out in that way.

Understanding of the principles of forecasting will not be impaired if we do not have access to a computer. Paper based exercises are more than adequate. However, do not expect to be able to apply the principles fully and productively to real work using paper only.

Using a computer – where to start

This section is intended for those who have never before touched a computer, or need to acquire one, or have no perception of how to apply them to forecasting.

It is not very long – and probably easier than you think.

Equipment required
All that is needed is a computer, a printer and a spreadsheet package. It is probably best to choose the spreadsheet software package first. There are three or four 'world leading' spreadsheet packages; you should ideally choose one of those. Before you buy it, you must ask a computer supplier to tell you what sort of machine will be needed to run it.

If your company already uses computers, it would be preferable to have one which was compatible with the others, or in other words, one capable of running the same sort of software.

If you are starting from scratch, there is little point in deviating from the current industry standard. Your computer supplier can advise you on this.

Learning how to use the computer and spreadsheet
Having obtained a computer and spreadsheet software, you
should expect to spend two or three days becoming
acquainted with as much as you need to get started. All
good computers come complete with manuals, and the
spreadsheet software will probably have a tutor built into it.

It is a very good idea during learning to have in mind a
small exercise to complete. The manuals and tutor will
probably cover far more than you need initially, and the best
way to learn, without a doubt, is through finding out how to
perform the functions necessary for our task.

**REMEMBER, THOUGH, THAT IT IS NOT NECESSARY
TO LEARN HOW TO USE A COMPUTER BEFORE
READING ON.**

If, however, you are already acquainted with computers and their spreadsheets, you may like to use them to set up some of the examples we will be looking at.

Budget and cash flow proforma on paper

The way in which basic budget and cash flow forecasts are structured on paper need be no different to their computer equivalents.

Your task will be made easier if you:

- use faint squared paper, at least 25 cm wide
- do not try to squash everything onto one sheet
- use a soft pencil, *not* a pen (a rubber is essential)
- have a large display desktop calculator to hand
- work in 'round' numbers: thousands, hundreds or tens
- allow good margins top and left for headings
- provide space on the right for totals and comments

Also, you should:

> • design and draw the layout and then photocopy it and enter figures on the copy

This way, if you change your mind about the layout, you will still have the 'master' without figures to work on.

Alternatively, there are pre-printed proforma available. Most of the major banks, as part of their service to small businesses, can supply them for budgets and cash flow. These have the advantages of saving you from working out a layout yourself, and most importantly, ensuring that details the bank require have been included. However, they may not be suitable for the on-going control that will be needed.

Summary

Today we have:

- seen that there are as many uses for budget forecasts as we can imagine.
- noted that cash flow forecasts are absolutely essential if the budget owner is concerned with cash flow, but may otherwise be unnecessary.
- understood what a spreadsheet is, whether paper or computer based.
- recognised that computer based forecasts have many advantages over paper versions, most significantly:

- absolute arithmetical accuracy
- ease of update and use for business plan modelling
- speed
- ease of chart production
- lower cost

- realised that starting up with a computer will not take long, and that a specific task is the best way to learn.

Preparing to build a forecast

Today we are looking at preparation for building a budget and cash flow forecast.

- Deciding our specific requirements
- Single or departmental forecasts
- The necessity of a cash flow forecast
- Deciding cost and income line headings

Like many things, the effort put into preparation will be more than repaid by reducing the number of subsequent changes to the forecast that will be necessary.

The first task is to decide, with colleagues, exactly what we are setting out to achieve with our forecast.

Deciding our specific requirements

Yesterday we saw that forecasts have many uses, and that they may be tailored to our precise needs.

Almost certainly we will not want to make use of every one of the facilities that were listed. And possibly, we will have a requirement that was not listed at all.

For example, profitability (which is listed) is unlikely to feature as relevant in the budget for the general administration department of a large company, because it does not have an income of its own.

The budget of that department will be concerned only with expenditure. It will be used first to determine how much needs to be spent, and when. Then it will be used to monitor and control expenditure by the department, and ensure that budget allocations are not exceeded.

On the other hand, a business with high stock turnover, such as a retailer, will certainly want to include the impact of stock levels (which is not listed) in the forecasts.

So is it possible to devise one budget and cash flow forecast structure which would serve all possible requirements by providing every possible facility?

In theory, the answer is almost YES, because if we could imagine all possible requirements, then we ought to be able to create a forecast which matched them. In reality, the answer is an absolute NO.

Why? First, every business is different from every other, and every business is likely to alter in some way over a period of time.

Second, any forecast designed to cater for a great many different requirements would be unimaginably complex, and quite impractical as an everyday management tool.

The practical way forward is to decide what the requirements are and design a forecast that addresses them.

For ease of understanding, it would be best to concentrate for the rest of the week on the specific example of an imaginary company. We can then highlight any significant exceptions for other cases as they arise.

The example business is called Widget Makers Ltd. It is a manufacturing company with just one product – the widget.

Managing Director

Production Manager   Sales Manager   Admin. Manager

We are the Managing Director (MD) and have overall responsibility for the company. We carry out forecasting ourselves, with the assistance of the other three managers.

The Admin. Manager is responsible for book-keeping and wages, and we will be working closely together when we look at detailed costs and revenues.

The Sales Manager is responsible for obtaining and forecasting widget sales.

The Production Manager is responsible for manufacturing widgets to fulfil the sales orders, and hence for forecasting parts and labour requirements.

Production labour consists of skilled full-time staff, and part-time unskilled workers taken on as and when required by production volumes.

All other staff are full-time.

We are discussing with the other managers what we need from our forecast, and how to structure it. It is most important that we listen carefully to their needs and comments.

The first job is to write down what we want our forecast to do, based on what we collectively want to achieve.

We decide that our forecast is needed principally for:

- forecasting production volumes against sales
- budgeting expenditure against revenue
- assessing profitability
- managing cash flow

Now, should we have a separate forecast for each department, or a single one for the whole company?

Single or departmental forecasts?

By 'a separate forecast for each department', we mean one that is a physically separate entity and which is constructed and controlled by the departmental head. One implication of this is that formal links between the different forecasts would have to be established.

For example, managers would agree the form and periodicity of sales forecast volumes updates from Sales to Production, and also to Admin and the MD.

Factors which affect our decision include:

- Will a single forecast be unmanageably large?
- Are separate departmental forecasts essential?
- Do we (the MD) want full visibility for ourselves?

In the case of Widget Makers Ltd, which is a small company, a single forecast is probably the best choice. It will not be unmanageably large and there is no reason why each of the managers should not have their own copy of the master forecast for reference.

If this is the first properly structured forecast that we are building, it will also be useful for us to have full visibility and control so that we can more easily recognise when changes and adjustments to it become necessary.

If we were managing a department of a larger company, the decision making process here would be very similar, except that we would certainly have to establish links with other departments and with the next level up the budget hierarchy.

The necessity of a cash flow forecast

There is no doubt whatever that Widget Makers Ltd need a cash flow forecast. They are a complete and self-contained entity, with a cash flow that will be strongly influenced by the peaks and troughs of production volumes.

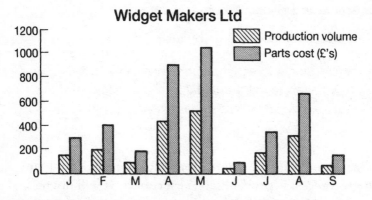

This chart illustrates a relationship between production volumes and the cost of parts to manufacture the volume.

The structure of the cash flow forecast will be determined almost entirely by that of the budget forecast. So, other than recognising that it will be necessary, we can safely leave consideration of it until we have finished the structure of the budget.

However, it would be useful at this point to deliberate on the circumstances in which a cash flow forecast is not essential.

A cash flow forecast may not be essential when:

- the budget is only part of a whole and cash flow is controlled at a higher level. A department of a large company, for example.
- there is no income and all expenditure is managed elsewhere. For instance, the Personnel Department of a larger company.
- cash outflow is simple and very regular, and not affected by business volumes. For example, a one man business with only overhead costs, which are all spread evenly throughout the year.

But we must be careful. Just because we do not have direct control of cash does not necessarily mean in itself that a cash flow forecast would not be useful. The discipline of recognising and understanding the cash flow of our budget can help us to play our part in the overall cash flow of the company. And we may find it useful as part of a presentation to our boss, in which we are bidding for some new equipment, for example.

Deciding cost and income headings

Having decided to have a single budget and cash flow for Widget Makers Ltd, we now need to establish the headings against which we can allocate all items of cost and income.

The number of headings should be sufficient to give us useful detail, but not so many that we are swamped with too much information.

For instance, most businesses will need more cost detail than these:

- Rent
- Stationery
- All other costs

At the opposite extreme, stationery broken down to these headings would be far too detailed for most businesses:

- Paper clips
- Pencils
- Elastic bands
- Envelopes
- Paper
- Staples

Every business is different and headings ideal for one may be useless to another. Before deliberating on them further, we should first consider the relationship of our budget to the company's book-keeping system and its nominal ledger.

Nominal ledger codes
Briefly, in book-keeping there is a ledger known as the
'nominal ledger'. The detail of its use need not concern us,
except to note that every item of expenditure and income is
recorded in it against a heading and reference number,
which together are known as the 'nominal code' or 'N/C'.

Now, it is often said that there is only one certainty in
forecasting, which is 'The forecast is wrong'.

This is absolutely true, and it is our task to review the
forecast and make adjustments as necessary to minimise the
inaccuracies.

Therefore:

> A fundamental requirement of a forecast is an ability to
> check its accuracy by comparing it with 'actual' data.

Comparing the forecast with actual data
Where does the 'actual' data come from? It can be obtained
by means of any special procedure that we may care to set
up, or it can come from the nominal ledger of the book-
keeping system.

Clearly, in a small business with just one budget forecast, it
would be sensible to use exactly the same headings that are
in the nominal ledger. If we are just starting up the
business, then we can simply allocate the same headings to
both. Because forecast and actual data are collected under
exactly the same headings, it is a simple matter to extract the
actual figures from the nominal ledger each month, and
compare them with the forecast.

In a larger company, the nominal codes used in the central book-keeping may be too broad for our purpose if we are just one department amongst many. In this case, we can decide our own headings as sub-sets of the company codes. We should, of course, do this in concert with the Accounts Department responsible for the book-keeping.

In summary, then:

- If the most convenient source of actual data is the nominal ledger, use the nominal codes as headings.
- If it is not possible or desirable to obtain actual data from the nominal ledger, we must decide headings for ourselves and set up a procedure for collecting actual figures under the same headings.

Use these checklists to choose suitable headings:

Cost headings
- Every monthly item which is 0.5% or more of the total
- Every item payable quarterly or annually
- No more than 30 headings

Income headings
- Sales per major item or groups of items
- Royalties
- Commission
- No more than 30 headings

Remember that every heading used means that we must be able to collect actual figures for it each month.

- If there are **too many** headings, it will be difficult to collect actual figures in the same form..

And we should remember that we will need to review and probably adjust our forecast each month.

- If there are **too few** headings, it will be difficult to find out what adjustments need to be made in the light of actual figures.

We will use these cost headings for Widget Makers Ltd:

Rent	Stationery	Full-time wages
Rates	Postage	Part-time wages
Salaries	Capital – cars	Tooling
Electricity	Insurance	Parts for widgets
Gas (heating)	Vehicle	Machine
	maintenance	maintenance
Telephone	Petrol	Other costs

and just two income headings:

Widget Mk 1 Sales
Widget MK 2 Sales

Now that we have decided the headings we will be using for our costs, we will need to look more closely at different categories of them, and decide how to arrange them in a logical order on our forecast.

We will do that tomorrow, and then return to our list of cost headings and assign a category to each one on Thursday.

Summary

Today, in preparing to build our forecast, we have:

- decided our specific requirements in co-operation with our colleagues, based upon:

  - the general requirements of all users of the forecast
  - a shortlist of the specific facilities they need
  - the pros and cons of single or departmental budgets

- noted that there is no doubt whatever that Widget Makers Ltd need a cash flow forecast. They are a

complete and self-contained entity, with a cash flow
that will be strongly influenced by the peaks and
troughs of production volumes.

- understood that there may be circumstances in which a
cash flow forecast is not essential, but that we should
think very carefully before dismissing one altogether.
- thought about the cost and income headings we should
use for our forecast, bearing in mind that:

- Too many headings generate ineffective detail
- Too few headings make comparison with actual
figures and subsequent adjustment difficult

Cost categories

Today we will consider various categories of cost:

Cost categories
- Capital costs
- Start-up costs
- Overhead costs
- Constant direct costs
- Variable direct costs

The category of an item of cost is determined chiefly by what it is used for, rather than what it is.

Generally, in this area more than any other, the 'rules' are really guidelines. Consider your fundamental use for each item of expense and allocate a category according to your needs.

For this reason, the examples given are illustrative only.

Capital costs

Definition
Capital costs are those expended on **fixed assets**.

Fixed assets are items having monetary value, which can be realised by selling them, and which are not consumed by the product.

What is this category for?
Capital costs are usually excluded from profitability calculations, so we need to be able to separate them from other costs or put them only in the cash flow forecast.

Examples of capital costs
- Buildings
- Machinery
- Vehicles
- Photocopiers
- Office furniture
- Computers

How do we handle these in our budget?
If we choose to include capital costs in our budget, and not just in the cash flow forecast, they should be clearly isolated from other expenses. A separate line on the budget for capital expenses is essential, and if it is useful to us, one line for each type of item: buildings, machinery, etc. Group all capital cost lines together.

Because we also want to know what the total expenditure is, including capital, we will need two 'total expenses' lines on our budget: one that includes capital costs and one that does not. We can then use whichever is appropriate.

Special Cases and Exceptions

1 If there are start-up costs as well as capital costs, the 'includes' total expenses line should combine both.

2 It could be argued that because an office kettle can be sold and its value realised, that it is a capital expense. Strictly speaking it is, but in practice most companies decide on a minimum level of expenditure which will be regarded as capital.

Start-up costs

Definition
Start-up costs are those associated with the introduction of a
new business or product. They are 'once only' expenses in
the sense that they are not part of the normal and on-going
cost of the new business or product.

They do not necessarily occur in the first week or month; it
could be some time into a new project before one arises. It is
the non-repeating nature of the cost which determines that it
is a 'start-up', not when it takes place.

What is this category for?
For exactly the same reason as we have a capital cost
category, but to deal with any non-capital items that we
want to exclude from profitability calculations.

Examples of start-up costs
- Special training
- Professional fees
- Bespoke computer software
- Introduction of a new pattern or mould
- Labour to rearrange a production line
- Design of revised sales literature

How do we handle these in our budget?
Start-up costs may be excluded from the budget and entered
only in the cost flow forecast. If we do want to include them
in the budget they should have a separate line, and if it is
useful to us, one line for each type of item.

Because we also want to know what the total expenditure is, including start-up costs, two 'total expenses' lines will be needed on the budget: one that includes start-ups and one that does not. We can then use whichever is appropriate.

Special Cases and Exceptions

1   If there are capital costs as well as start-up costs, the 'includes' total expenses line should combine both.

2   If we choose not to identify start-up costs separately, then they should be grouped with either overhead or constant direct costs.

3   Some costs initially thought of as start-up may also be capital costs. For the purpose of forecasting it makes no difference which category we use, but for financial accounting capital cost is preferred. Check with an accountant if in doubt.

Overhead costs

Definition
Overhead costs are expenses not directly related to the product. (Overheads are sometimes called indirect costs.)

Looking at it another way, if production of the product ceased for a period of, say, a month or two or stopped altogether, would the expense still exist? If the answer is yes, then it should probably be regarded as an overhead cost.

What is this category for?
It is very important to understand which costs are not directly associated with the product, so that:

- we know which will not be affected by product volume changes
- if there is more than one product, the overheads can be properly apportioned between them if we wish
- we can calculate the profitability of individual products

Examples of overhead costs
- Rent
- Rates
- Heating and lighting
- The wages department
- Maintenance of the photocopier
- Pay costs of staff not directly involved with the product

How do we handle these in our budget?
Include a heading for each significant overhead item and group them all together.

Special cases and exceptions
In a department of a larger company, there may be no overhead costs controlled by the department. However, the company may have a policy of distributing overheads throughout all departments.

In this case, overhead costs, either as a number of lines or grouped as a single figure, might be dictated to the department. If so, simply include those figures in the budget, but exclude them from the cash flow forecast, because we will not be paying the bills for them.

Alternatively, the company may choose not to provide any overhead cost figures at all. No problem; simply ignore the category altogether.

Constant direct costs

Definition
Constant direct costs are those associated directly with the product but which are unaffected by changes in product volume.

If production of the product ceased for a week and the expense item remained unchanged for that period, then it would probably be regarded as a constant direct.

What is this category for?
It is important to understand which costs exist *only* because a product exists. This is especially true in a multi-department or multi-product company where it is desirable to:

- establish the individual profitability of each product or department
- properly assess the impact of adding a new product or department, or removing one altogether
- understand to what extent the profitability of an individual product or department is limited by non-volume related costs

> **Examples of constant direct costs**
> - The pay costs of a production line supervisor
> - The pay costs of full time production line staff
> - Routine maintenance of production line machines

How do we handle these in our budget?
Group all constant direct cost lines together.

Special cases and exceptions
In a smaller company with just one budget, it may be difficult to distinguish between overheads and constant directs. If so, the solution is to use just one of the categories – overheads would probably be best.

Variable direct costs

Definition
Variable direct costs are those directly associated with the product and which vary with the production volumes.

If production volumes change and there is a consequential variation in the expense, then it should be regarded as a variable direct cost. The consequential variation need not necessarily be in direct proportion to the volume change.

What is this category for?
The importance of this category is in direct proportion to the percentage of costs allocated to it. For instance, a manufacturing business's expenses are very much affected by the amount of raw material it buys. If production doubles, material costs are likely to increase by the same proportion.

It is therefore essential to successful forecasting that variable direct costs are identified and quantified.

Examples of variable direct costs
- Materials used in manufacture
- Labour employed only as required
- Power for production machinery
- Wasted production material
- Delivery vehicle fuel
- Spare parts for a maintenance service

How do we handle these in our budget?
These costs, by definition, are going to vary according to the product volume forecast. They are dependent on it.

There will be an arithmetical relationship between the product volume and each variable direct cost, and this must be included in the budget.

For example, suppose that the parts to make one widget cost £1.75. The arithmetic relationship is simply:

Number of widgets x £1.75

The budget should have a line labelled 'parts cost per widget' and another labelled 'total widget parts expense'.

Note that we are using the interchangeable terms 'cost' and 'expense' to help distinguish between cost per item, and the cost of a group, or groups, of items.

After entering 'parts cost per widget', multiply it by the 'forecast widget production' volume in the corresponding column, and the result goes in the 'total widget parts expense' line. Like this:

	Jan	Feb	Mar	Apr ...etc
Forecast widget production	100	150	200	50
Parts cost per widget (£)	1.75	1.75	1.50	2.00
Total widget parts expense (£)	175.00	262.50	300.00	100.00

Notice that we have forecast a reduction of £0.25 for buying parts in March, and an increase of £0.25 in April, to reflect the discount structure the supplier applies to the quantity bought at any one time.

In practice, there will normally be many individually priced items which together form the total variable direct cost.

Whether they are all treated individually or grouped together is at the discretion of the forecaster. For example, this:

	Jan	Feb	Mar	Apr ..etc
Forecast widget production	100	150	200	50
Minor part A cost (£)	1.00	1.00	1.00	1.00
Minor part B cost (£)	.50	.50	.50	.50
Minor part C cost (£)	1.20	1.20	1.20	1.20
Major part cost (£)	20.00	20.00	20.00	20.00
Minor part A expense (£)	100.00	150.00	200.00	50.00
Minor part B expense (£)	50.00	75.00	100.00	25.00
Minor part C expense (£)	120.00	180.00	240.00	60.00
Major part expense (£)	2000.00	3000.00	4000.00	1000.00
Total widget parts expense (£)	2270.00	3405.00	4540.00	1135.00

could be simplified by using the total cost of all three of the minor parts, like so:

	Jan	Feb	Mar	Apr...etc
Forecast widget production	100	150	200	50
All minor parts cost(£)	2.70	2.70	2.70	2.70
Major part cost(£)	20.00	20.00	20.00	20.00
All minor parts expense(£)	270.00	405.00	540.00	135.00
Major part expense(£)	2000.00	3000.00	4000.00	1000.00
Total widget parts expense(£)	2270.00	3405.00	4540.00	1135.00

Criteria for deciding what to combine and what to separate in variable direct costs include:

- The likely amount of variation in price for each item. A large variation suggests grouping is not appropriate.
- Are the proportions of the arithmetic relationships with product volume the same? For instance, if there is always one of Item A used for a widget, no matter what quantity of widgets are being made, but a gradually increasing number of Item B used as widget production quantities rise, then it would not be appropriate to group Items A and B together.
- It is useful to keep different kinds of variable direct costs apart, for instance labour and materials.

Special cases and exceptions
It is quite possible for a business to have no variable direct costs, or for any to be so insignificant that it is easiest to combine them with another category.

Examples of this include company departments or self-employed consultants whose product is 'answering queries' or 'giving advice'. The consultant might use a little more paper and coffee if he is busier than normal, but the additional expense is insignificantly small compared to his overheads of office rent, telephone and car.

Summary

We should not expect to be able to absorb all of today's work in one reading, but we can easily refer back to it as and when necessary.

The fundamental points to bear in mind are:

- Cost categories are essential to good forecasting.
- There are just five types:

  - Capital costs
  - Start-up costs
  - Overhead costs
  - Constant direct costs
  - Variable direct costs

- We categorise according to what an item is used **for**.

The structure of the forecast

Today we are going to design the structure and layout of the budget and cash flow forecasts. We will be looking at:

- Allocating cost categories
- Choosing the forecasting period
- Layout and structure of the budget
- Layout and structure of the cash flow

Allocating cost categories

On Tuesday we made a list of the cost headings that would be used for Widget Makers Ltd forecast. We will now assign categories to each of the headings according to the principles discussed on Wednesday.

This was the list of headings for Widget Makers Ltd:

Rent	Stationery	Full-time wages
Rates	Postage	Part-time wages
Salaries	Vehicles	Tooling
Electricity	Insurance	Parts for widgets
Gas (heating)	Vehicle maintenance	Machine maintenance
Telephone	Petrol	Other costs

We will take each of the cost categories in turn, and decide which of the headings to assign to them.

Just to remind ourselves, the cost categories are:

- Capital
- Start-up
- Overhead
- Constant direct
- Variable direct

The definition under each category below is intended as a brief reminder. Refer back to Wednesday for a more detailed explanation.

Capital costs
These are items having monetary value, which can be realised by selling them. They are sometimes called fixed assets. They are usually excluded from calculations of profitability.

We only have one capital cost heading: **Vehicles**

Start-up costs
These are any non-repeating costs associated with a new
business or project. A start-up cost might also be a capital
item, in which case capital is probably best. Like capital,
start-up costs are usually excluded from profit calculations.

We have only one start-up cost: **Tooling**

Overhead costs
These are costs not directly related to the product.

Our overhead costs are: **Rent   Stationery   Salaries
Rates   Postage   Insurance
Telephone**

Constant direct costs
These are costs directly related to the product, but which are
not significantly affected by changes in product volumes.

Our constant direct costs are: **Full-time wages
Gas (heating) #
Vehicle maintenance *
Machine maintenance**

\#   Although the gas heating also serves the office areas, 95%
of the cost is for the factory space. It is then quite
satisfactory to allocate the total amount for gas to
constant direct costs.

*   The vehicle is a widget delivery van. If it were a
manager's car for their personal use, its maintenance
would be categorised as an overhead.

Variable direct costs

These costs are directly related to the product and fluctuate according to product volume.

These are our variable direct costs: **Part-time wages**
Electricity ##
Parts for widgets
Petrol **

\# \# Although a little electricity is used for lighting and other minor purposes in the offices, a great deal more is used by the operation of the widget making machines.

** The widget delivery van's mileage is largely dependent upon the volume of production, and hence deliveries. If the petrol was for a manager's car it would be allocated to overheads.

Right, that is all of the headings, except one: **Other**

Inevitably, there will be costs that do not belong to any of the headings, but which are so small that they do not warrant a heading of their own. These costs should be collectively allocated to 'Other'.

But to which category should 'Other' be allocated?

In practice it will be found that most of the categories need an 'Other' heading, if not immediately then at some time in the future. It is therefore best to assume that this will be the case and put an 'Other' heading with each category.

Choosing the forecasting period

Budgets are usually prepared to span 12 months, although there is no reason why they cannot be for a longer term if that is what is required. We will work on 12 months.

The 12 months may be divided into any period that suits us. The most usual are either calendar months – 12 periods per year, or 4-weekly – 13 periods per year.

In some businesses a weekly period might be the most suitable, where for instance sales volume or cash flow or both are subject to wide fluctuation and a monthly forecast would conceal essential detail. But remember that detail in the forecast is only of real use if you are able to compare actual figures with it on a very similar basis.

Another practical concern of forecasting with weekly periods is the number of arithmetic calculations, and the physical size of the spreadsheet. These pose no problem at all for a computer based forecast, but on paper they are really so significant that weekly periods should not be considered as a practical option.

Most businesses find that either 12 or 13 periods per year will meet their requirements and again, the principal deciding factor is simply the need to compare the forecast with actual figures. If actual figures are to be drawn from the company ledgers and these are kept on a calendar month basis, then the forecast should have 12 periods per year.

If we have our own business, we can start the budget (or financial year) at any convenient date we choose. Some British companies start with April to line up with the tax year.

A department of a company, or a subsidiary, will use the same financial year as other departments of their parent company.

For our purposes we will use a financial year which starts on January 1st, divided into 12 periods of calendar months.

Widget Makers Ltd – the forecasting year and periods

Months	Jan	Feb	Mar	Apr	May	Jun	Jul	Aug	Sep	Oct	Nov	Dec
Periods	1	2	3	4	5	6	7	8	9	10	11	12

Layout of the budget

We are now at the stage where we can design the layout of our forecasts.

Do not expect to get them right first time; inevitably your ideas will develop as you go along and changes will be made. This presents no difficulty at all if a computer is being used but can be onerous on paper. There are some suggestions to ease the way for designing layouts on paper at the end of Monday's chapter.

The heading sections that we need are determined by our basic requirements. We decided those for Widget Makers Ltd on Tuesday; they were:

- Forecasting production volumes against sales
- Budgeting expenditure against revenue
- Assessing profitability
- Managing cash flow

We also decided to have a single forecast, rather than a separate one for each department.

Widget Makers Ltd budget forecast
Now, we have a simple decision to make here, based on a couple of general rules:

Rule 1   If, for any reason, there will not be a cash flow forecast, then *every* item of expenditure and income will appear on the budget forecast.

Rule 2   On the other hand, if there will be a cash flow forecast, then any item of expenditure and income that we choose to exclude from calculations of profitability can be excluded from the budget and included on the cash flow.

Rule 2 is not absolutely rigid. We could if we wished include all items of expenditure and income on the budget and simply exclude them from the calculations of profit.

We will use Rule 2 for our purposes as MD of Widget Makers Ltd.

The primary section headings that will be needed on the budget are:

**** INCOME ****

Sales revenue

**** EXPENSE ****

Variable direct
Constant direct
Overhead

Capital and start-up expenditure will be excluded from the profitability calculations, and so will be put in the cash flow forecast later on.

The order of the list is logical in terms of the particular budget, although certainly not the only logical possibility. It really makes no difference at all what the order is, save to say that interpretation of it by every user should be easy.

Now the income and cost headings can be inserted in each of the category sections, according to our allocation of them.

Inserting the income and cost headings

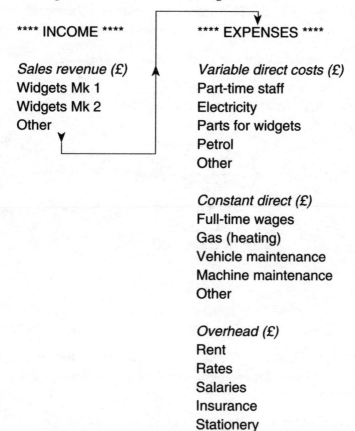

**** INCOME ****

Sales revenue (£)
Widgets Mk 1
Widgets Mk 2
Other

**** EXPENSES ****

Variable direct costs (£)
Part-time staff
Electricity
Parts for widgets
Petrol
Other

Constant direct (£)
Full-time wages
Gas (heating)
Vehicle maintenance
Machine maintenance
Other

Overhead (£)
Rent
Rates
Salaries
Insurance
Stationery
Postage
Telephone
Other

Now some additional rows need to be inserted, in which we
can enter the figures that will enable any income or expense
related to sales volume to be calculated.

Inserting the rows for volume related items, and for sub-totals and totals

**** INCOME ****

Sales volume (Qty)
Widgets Mk 1
Widgets Mk 2
Other

Sales rates (£/item)
Widgets Mk 1
Widgets Mk 2
Other

Sales revenue (£)
Widgets Mk 1
Widgets Mk 2
Other
    Total sales revenue

**** EXPENSES ****

*Variable direct volumes
(Qty)*
Part-time staff
Electricity
Parts for widgets
Petrol
Other

*Variable direct rates
(£/item)*
Part-time staff
Electricity
Parts for widgets
Petrol
Other

Variable direct costs (£)
Part-time staff
Electricity
Parts for widgets
Petrol
Other
    Subtotal

Constant direct (£)
Full-time wages
Gas (heating)
Vehicle maintenance
Machine maintenance
Other
    Subtotal

Overhead (£)
Rent
Rates
Salaries
Insurance
Stationery
Postage
Telephone
Other
    Subtotal

    Total expenses

Finally, add the profit and break-even line headings, lines for VAT, and the budget format is complete. A list of the full set of headings is given in Appendix 1.

Layout of the cash flow

There are fundamentally two layout methods which can be used to present the cash flow forecast:

1   Include every heading which is on the budget forecast.
2   Include only the subtotal and totals from the budget forecast.

Either layout can be used if you are using a computer spreadsheet. If you are using paper spreadsheets, then only the first is practical. The reason for this will become clear when we consider forecast reviews.

Both methods will also need any items of cash flow which are not shown on the budget forecast.

Method 1
The cash flow forecast will have all of the (£) headed sections from the budget, and all of their row headings.

In addition we will need any items of cash out and cash in that have been excluded from the budget, such as capital and start-up. For illustration, we will add two more headings:

'Bank loan' to the cash in section
'Loan repayment' to the cash out section

Bank account rows will also be needed.

Here are the cash flow forecast lines for Method 1:

CASH IN
Sales ....
Widgets Mk 1 ....
Widgets Mk 2 ....
Other ....

Subtotal ..

Other
Bank loan ....

Subtotal ..

Total cash in ..

CASH OUT

Capital
Vehicles...........................
Other ....

Subtotal ..

Start-up
Tooling ....
Other ....

Subtotal ..

Other
Loan repayment ....

Subtotal ..

Variable direct
Part-time staff ....
Electricity ....
Parts for widgets ....
Petrol ....
Other ....

Subtotal ..

Constant direct
Full-time wages ....
Gas (heating) ....
Vehicle maintenance ....
Machine maintenance .....
Other ....

Subtotal ..

Overhead
Rent.................................
Rates ....
Salaries ....
Insurance ....
Stationery ....
Postage ....
Telephone ....
Other ....

Subtotal ..

Total cash out ..

Bank
Opening balance ....
Cash in ....
Cash out ....
Closing balance...............

Net cash flow...................

A list of the full set of headings is given in Appendix 1.

Method 2

Method 2 is very much simpler; it looks like this:

CASH IN
From the budget ....
Bank loan ....

Total cash in ..

CASH OUT
Other
Vehicles ....
Tooling ....
Loan repayment ....

Subtotal ..

From the budget

Variable direct Subtotal ..

Constant direct Subtotal ..

Overhead   Subtotal ..

Total cash out ..

BANK
Opening balance ....
Cash in ....
Cash out ....
Closing balance ....

Net Cash Flow ....

That then completes most of what we need to know about the structure and layout of the forecasts. On Friday we will be looking at calculations on the forecasts, and at the kind of spreadsheet links we will need if we are using a computer.

Also on Friday we will consider how VAT can be dealt with.

Summary

Today, in designing our forecasts, we have:

- allocated each cost heading to one of the cost categories, remembering that we should categorise costs according to what the cost is for, not what it is.
- decided to use a forecasting period of 12 calendar months, but noted that we could also have used either 13 4-weekly periods, or 52 one-week periods for the year.
- excluded capital and start-up costs from the budget forecast to simplify profitability calculations, but of course included them on the cash flow forecast.
- chosen to use a cash flow forecast layout which includes all of the budget line headings. We noted that this layout (Method 1) is suitable for either computer or paper spreadsheets, but that the simpler layout (Method 2) is only suitable for computerised versions.

Putting the figures in

- The arithmetic
- Handling VAT
- Identifying and quantifying costs
- Linking the budget and cash flow

We have established the layout of the forecasts, but before the budget figures are entered we need to take care of the spreadsheet arithmetic, and then decide what to do about the VAT part of costs and income.

After the budget figures have been put in, we will consider the spreadsheet links in the case of a computer version.

The arithmetic

It is a good idea, especially when just starting out on forecasts, to clearly show how the more complex calculated figures are arrived at. This should be regardless of whether a paper or computer spreadsheet is being used.

Not only will we find it helpful, but it will also make understanding by someone else very much easier.

Here are the calculations for the income part of the budget forecast.

**** INCOME ****

Sales volume (Qty)	Sales rates (£)	Sales revenue (£)
Widgets Mk 1... [A] x	Widgets Mk 1.. =	Widgets Mk 1... [D]
Widgets Mk 2... [B] x	Widgets Mk 2.. =	Widgets Mk 2... [E]
Other................ [C] x	Other.............. =	Other................ [F]

Total sales volume [G] = A + B + C
Total sales revenue [H] = D + E + F

The same principle can be used to illustrate the rest of the budget forecast calculations, but this time we will mark only the subtotals of the sections.

**** EXPENSES ****

Variable direct (£) Subtotal .. [J]

*Constant direct (£)*Subtotal .. [K]

Subtotal direct expenses (£) [L] = (J + K)

Gross profit
Amount ... [M] = (H - L)
As a % return on sales .... [N] = (M ÷ H x 100)
Amount per item sold .... [P] = (M ÷ G)

Overhead (£) Subtotal .. [R]

Total expenses (£) .... [S] = (L + R)

Net profit (excl. tax)
Amount .... [T] = (M - R)
Amount per sale .... [U] = (T ÷ G)
As a % return on sales .... [V] = (T ÷ H x 100)

Break-even calculations
Value of sales .... [W] = (R ÷ N x 100)
Volume of sales .... [X] = (W x G ÷ H)

That then is the arithmetic of the budget forecast.

The arithmetic of a cash flow forecast, where no VAT is involved, is simply addition to subtotals and totals.

But if, like Widget Makers Ltd, we are concerned with VAT, then there is just a little more to do.

Handling VAT

Important note: VAT, although simple in concept, contains many detailed aspects that would be inappropriate to address here. **Do not make any decision concerning VAT without advice from HM Customs and Excise or a qualified professional such as an accountant**.

A company registered for VAT is required to charge VAT for any services or products they supply that are subject to the tax. The VAT they receive is then passed on to HM Customs and Excise, after first subtracting any VAT paid out in the course of the company's business.

The payments to HM Customs and Excise (known as the VAT return) are usually made quarterly, and are based on the dates on which invoices were issued.

There is also an alternative system known as the Cash Accounting Scheme which businesses not exceeding a specified turnover may apply for. VAT returns under this scheme are based on when cash is received and paid.

In either case the forecasting principles are the same. They are in three stages:

Stage 1
The first job is to calculate the value of 'VAT received in' as part of Cash In, and 'VAT paid out' as part of Cash Out. The rows for these have been included under 'Other' in each case in Appendix 1. The calculations are based only on those items subject to VAT. Wages for instance, are not subject to VAT. 'VAT received in' and 'VAT paid out' are **included** in Total Cash In and Total Cash Out.

Stage 2

The second job is to calculate the difference between the VAT charged on sales and the VAT charged when we make purchases.

If accounting with invoices, subtract 'VAT for expenses' from 'VAT for sales' in the budget forecast, and put the result in the line headed 'Net VAT' on the cash flow forecast. Note that this figure is **not** included in the Total Cash Out sum.

If accounting with cash, subtract the figure for 'VAT paid out' from 'VAT received in' on the cash flow forecast, and put the result in the 'Net VAT' line. Again note that this figure is **not** included in the Total Cash Out sum.

Stage 3

Now we need to calculate how much we will be sending to Customs and Excise each quarter. An example will help.

Let us suppose that one of our VAT quarters runs from April 1st to June 30th. This means that by the end of July we must send our VAT return off with any payment due.

The amount we owe (or are owed) for each month is now in the Net VAT line. So all we have to do in our column for July is to add the Net VAT figures for the preceding three months, in this case April, May and June.

The resulting figure is **included** in the Total Cash Out sum.

These calculations are illustrated on page 82.

The example illustrates the VAT invoice accounting method. VAT is calculated at 17.5%. We are assuming that cash is paid out in the same month as the purchase invoice date, and that cash is received one month after sales invoices were raised. During May there was significant additional expenditure, hence Net VAT is a minus quantity.

A cash accounting scheme example would be very similar, except that Net VAT would be calculated on 'VAT received' and 'VAT paid'.

If during a quarter the amount of VAT incurred on expenses is greater than the amount on sales, then of course the whole quarter's Net VAT will be a minus quantity. This means the amount is owed by HM Customs and Excise, which they will refund on receipt of the VAT return. The cash flow in the example automatically takes account of this.

Whilst registration for VAT is mandatory if a business's annual sales are expected to be greater than the currently legislated figure, voluntary registration may be applied for if sales are below it.

A small business with sales below the limit, whose customers are mainly other businesses that are registered for VAT, may well decide on voluntary registration. Because the VAT they would then have to charge will in effect be refunded to their customer by HM Customs and Excise, the additional cost of it will not effect their purchasing decision. On the other hand, if the small business's customers are mainly private individuals or small businesses not registered for VAT, who therefore cannot reclaim it, then they will probably decide against registering voluntarily.

VAT Example – invoice accounting
(Figures rounded to £'s)

BUDGET

	Mar	Apr	May	Jun	Jul	
Sales invoices [A]	800	2000	1200	1400	1000	(17.5% of sales subject to VAT)
VAT on sales	140	350	210	245	175	
Expense invoices [B]	710	950	1500	1050	750	(17.5% of expenses subject to VAT)
VAT on expenses	124	166	263	184	131	

CASH FLOW

	Mar	Apr	May	Jun	Jul	
Cash in		800	2000	1200	1400	(One month after sales invoice)
VAT received		140	350	210	245	(One month after sales invoice)
Total cash in		940	2350	1410	1645	
Cash out	710	950	1500	1050	750	(Same month as expense invoice)
VAT paid	124	166	263	184	131	(Same month as expense invoice)
Net VAT [A – B]	16	184	(53)	61	44	(**Not** included in Total Cash Out)
VAT return	#	#			192	(Sum of Net VAT in Apr, May and Jun)
Total Cash Out	#	1116	1763	1234	1073	

[# There are no figures before March in this example, so neither Cash In and Cash Out for March, nor a VAT return for April, are shown.]

Identifying and quantifying costs

We are now almost ready to enter the figures. Because most of the figures in the cash flow are derived directly from the budget forecast, we will start with the latter.

There are many different ways of identifying and quantifying costs, and which we use will depend upon our particular situation.

If there is an existing book-keeping system, then historic information from it is one of the most reliable sources.

Bank statements from the last two years or so can also be extremely useful sources of information, though of course we would have to analyse the records according to the cost and income headings we have chosen.

If we are in a department of a company with no historic book-keeping data available and no bank account, there may be information that has been kept in some other form. If not, then the task is much like that for a new business.

A new business has the advantage that right from the start it can ensure that the breakdown of costs and income is suitable for forecasting and performance monitoring.

Being honest with ourselves
In any event, first of all, we should think carefully about **why** we are doing this, and remember that it is principally for our own benefit as a manager. We are establishing a system that will give us clear information to enable us to make sound business decisions.

It is quite possible, however, that one of the first uses for the forecasts will be as supporting information for a business case to raise finance, or investment in some new project or equipment.

It is in these circumstances that we must be most careful.

We will find that once we have our figures in place, especially if they are on a computer, that just a little tweak here and a little tweak there can turn a projected large loss or overdraft into a healthy profit or bank balance. This of course is why the system will be one of our most powerful management tools. But like all powerful devices, they can also be dangerous.

The temptation may be there to put 'just a little tweak' in, and bias the forecast in favour of a pre-determined view or to support a slightly over-optimistic sales forecast.

But of course, in the end, we will have to deal with the consequences of this sort of action. We eventually fool nobody but ourselves.

The most objective forecast possible is what is needed. A forecast that understates profit is just as 'wrong' as one which overstates it. Nevertheless, it is wise to use the pessimistic end of a range of confidence limits, especially whilst the forecast is new and has not been tested in practice.

In summary, then, in identifying and quantifying costs, we should:

- use historic information from a book-keeping system wherever possible
- where there is no book-keeping data, look for other sources that will help to establish past trends
- be objective
- default to the 'worst case' figure where there is a range of options

We can now enter the figures on the budget forecast, using whole number values of an appropriate order. Many businesses will be able to work in thousands; precision to pence is unnecessary in any event. Most importantly, we should not mix orders. For example, if we have chosen to work in thousands we must be consistent; £250 would be entered as 0.25.

Linking the budget and cash flow

When using paper forecasts, the links between the budget and cash flow are only notional. But they must be exceptionally clear in our minds, because whenever we make a change to the budget forecast, we will have to make a corresponding change to the cash flow forecast.

When using a computer spreadsheet we should directly link the cash flow forecast to the budget. In this way any figures put into the budget will be automatically picked up by the cash flow. Clearly the links will need to be offset where necessary so that cash related to sales invoices, for instance, appears in the correctly forecasted month.

All that is left to complete data entry is to put any income or expenditure into the cash flow forecast that does not appear on the budget forecast, such as capital and start-up, bank loans and repayments.

The forecasts are now ready for use.

Summary

Today we completed our forecast structures and entered figures for the year.

We have seen:

- that it is very useful to clearly show the basis of our calculations.
- how VAT may be handled within our forecast, and noted the importance of taking professional advice on detailed aspects of VAT.
- the significance of objectivity in our forecast – we fool nobody but ourselves otherwise.
- that historic book-keeping data is the best source of trend information on which to base our forecast.
- how computer spreadsheet links between the budget and cash flow eliminate the need to transfer figures from one to the other, and that consequently any change to the budget will be automatically picked up in the cash flow forecast.

Finale

Now that we have completed our forecasts we will need to maintain them in good working order. Today we will be looking at forecast monitoring and review, and thinking about how much or little accuracy we need. Finally we will summarise our week's work.

- Monitoring and review
- Grand summary

Monitoring and review

Before the days of desktop computers, budget forecasts, if they existed at all, were on paper, and it was common for them to be prepared just once a year. This of course meant that any detailed review could only be carried out once a year, and clearly much could have changed during that time.

The advent of computer spreadsheets makes more frequent reviews not only possible and easy, but also positively encourages them. We will find that we await arrival of the period end actual figures with eager anticipation, because we will be able to see how accurate our forecast was for the last month, and whether we will be able to make any adjustments to the coming months' forecasts.

What then are we going to do with the 'actual' figures for the month?

First, we will want to compare them with our forecast, certainly for the period in question, and possibly as cumulative 'year-to-date' figures.

Second, we may want to revise the forecast ahead, either because actual trends indicate an inaccurate assumption, or because there is a change in business volumes or policy.

If we are using a paper spreadsheet, our options for how we do this are limited. A method commonly used in the past was to split each month's column into two and put the forecast figures in one of them. The other column was then used for recording and comparing actual figures. If cumulative year-to-date comparisons were also required, then it was probably best to have a separate forecast sheet that showed cumulative figures in the forecast half of the column, and again actual cumulative data could be entered in the other.

Computer spreadsheets provide a wide range of possibilities. We will look at the outline principles of just two, plus a combination of both.

Overwrite method
One of the simplest ways to record actual figures is to overwrite the forecast; literally to replace whatever the forecast figure was with the actual.

Aspects and limitations of this method are:

- It is necessary to consider how actual figures will affect calculations and links between budget and cash flow when the forecast structure and layout is designed.
- Comparison with the original forecast-to-date cannot be carried out with the computer, although printouts of earlier versions can be used for this in many cases.

Dual forecast method
For this method, an additional copy of the original forecast is made (it only takes a few seconds) in such a way that the first may be kept unaltered as a record of the original. Actual figures are then overwritten into the copy.

Aspects and limitations of this method are:

- Because there is a permanent computer record of the original forecast, comparisons of period and cumulative figures may be carried out using the computer directly.
- This system is very well suited to budgets which are absolutely fixed for the year, and for which the prime purpose of the forecast is to monitor adherence to the cost and income allocations.

Combination method

This method is a combination of overwrite and dual forecast.

Often a complete record of an original budget is not required for comparison purposes, but just one or two key headings, for example, Total Sales Volume and Total Cost.

To be able to compare the original forecast for these headings with actual figures, all we need do is make a copy of the appropriate rows only. We should of course remove any links in the copied rows, so that they do not automatically change when actual figures are used to overwrite.

Having retained unchangeable copies of the original forecast of Total Sales Volume and Total Cost, say, it is now easy to compare them with actual data as it is entered.

The combination method will probably suit most applications.

There is a list of useful figures and ratios in Appendix 2 that can be used when building and reviewing forecasts.

The week in summary

What are the key features of our week's work?

- Budget and cash flow forecasts are amongst the most valuable tools available to managers. They enable informed decisions to be made, and reduce the probability of hurried and reactive management.
- Forecasting is not the sole province of accountants. On the contrary, forecasts depend far more upon a clear understanding of the business than knowledge of accountancy or book-keeping.
- Forecasts, even if they are physically large, are not complicated. The best way to appreciate this is to prepare a forecast ourselves.
- We should assume that cash flow forecasts are always essential, and only dispense with them once absolutely convinced they are not relevant to a particular case.
- A computer-based spreadsheet is the only really practical basis for usable forecasts.
- We categorise costs according to what the expenditure is for, not what the item is.
- We choose cost and income headings specifically to address our needs. There will be enough to provide us with sufficient detail, but not so many that we are swamped with too much information.
- We can start our forecast year in any month we like, and will probably decide to use either 12 calendar month or 13 4-week periods in the year. Exceptionally, if our business requires it, we will use 52 one-week periods.

- Wherever possible forecast figures are based upon trends from a source of historic information, such as the book-keeping system.
- Forecasts are always wrong. Therefore they must be regularly reviewed for accuracy by comparing them with actual figures as they become available, and updated if necessary to reflect any changes to the forecast for the business.
- Most forecast applications will be suited to the 'combination method' for accepting actual figures. This enables comparison of the original forecast for key figures with the actual data, without the need for multiple copies of the forecast.

And finally, we must not forget our responsibilities when we start to use our forecasts for business plan evaluation, 'what if' analysis or other profit improving exercises.

Until our colleagues have learned what we have learned this week, we will know far more about the detail of the business, and far more about the consequences of any decisions and policies, than they do.

You are now in complete control: use your knowledge wisely.

Widget Makers Ltd – Forecast line and column headings

BUDGET FORECAST

	Jan	Feb

**** INCOME ****

Sales volume (Qty)
Widgets Mk 1
Widgets Mk 2
Other
Total sales volume

Sales rates (£)
Widgets Mk 1
Widgets Mk 2
Other

Sales revenue (£)
Widgets Mk 1
Widgets Mk 2
Other
Total sales revenue

VAT for sales

**** EXPENSES ****

Variable direct volumes (Qty)
Part-time staff
Electricity
Parts for widgets
Petrol
Other

Variable direct rates (£)
Part-time staff
Electricity
Parts for widgets
Petrol
Other

Variable direct costs (£)
Part-time staff
Electricity
Parts for widgets
Petrol
Other
Subtotal

BUDGET AND CASH FLOW

...Nov	Dec	Year	Avge	Cumulative	Jan	Feb ....

CASH FLOW FORECAST

**** CASH IN ****

Sales
Widgets Mk 1
Widgets Mk 2
Other
Subtotal

Other
Bank loan
VAT received in
Subtotal

Total Cash In

**** CASH OUT ****

Capital
Vehicles
Other
Subtotal

Start-up
Tooling
Other
Subtotal

Other
Loan repayment
VAT paid out
Subtotal

Variable direct

Part-time staff ....
Electricity ....
Parts for widgets ....
Petrol ....
Other ....
Subtotal ....

Constant direct

Full-time wages ....
Gas (heating) ....
Vehicle maintenance ....
Machine maintenance ....
Other ....
Subtotal ....

Overhead

Rent ....
Rates ....
Salaries ....
Insurance ....
Stationery ....
Postage ....
Telephone ....
Other ....
Subtotal ....

Customs and Excise

Net VAT (Exclude from total cash out) ....
VAT return – Payment/(Refund) ....
Total Cash Out ....

Bank

Opening balance ....
Cash in ....
Cash out ....
Closing balance ....

Net Cash Flow ....

Constant direct (£)

Full-time wages ....
Gas (heating) ....
Vehicle maintenance ....
Machine maintenance ....
Other ....
Subtotal ....
Sub total direct expenses ....

Gross profit

Amount ....
As a % return on sales ....
Amount per item sold ....

Overhead (£)

Rent ....
Rates ....
Salaries ....
Insurance ....
Stationery ....
Postage ....
Telephone ....
Other ....
Subtotal ....

VAT for expenses ....
Total expenses ....

Net Profit (excl. tax)

Amount ....
Amount per sale ....
As a % of sales ....

Break-even calculations

Value of sales ....
Volume of sales ....

Useful figures and ratios

A selection of figures and ratios that may be useful when reviewing a forecast, or testing 'what if' options.

All of these can be derived from the data that would exist in the example of Widget Makers Ltd.

Average cash flow
Average direct costs
Average sales
Average total cost
Direct cost/sale
Direct costs/direct employee
Direct costs: total costs
Gross profit as a percentage of sales
Gross profit/employee
Gross profit/sale
Net profit as a percentage of sales
Net profit per employee
Net profit/sale
Overhead cost/sale
Overhead costs/employee
Overhead costs: direct costs
Overhead costs: total costs
Sales/direct employee
Total cost/sale

In your own forecast, try playing with other ratios and averages and see whether they may be particularly useful.

Remember – every business is different.